The Trilogy of Surfaces and Invisibilities

Nora Gomringer

Translated by Annie Rutherford

Illustrations by Reimar Limmer

Burning Eye

BurningEyeBooks
Never Knowingly
Mainstream

Copyright © Nora Gomringer and Verlag Voland & Quist,
"Monster-Morbus-Moden" 2019

English translation copyright © 2022 Annie Rutherford

Illustrations by Reimar Limmer

"Seidenraupen" (page 139) is a detail of an embroidery by Daniela
Hoferer (Daniela Hoferer "Stream of Consciousness", 2016.
Copyright © Daniela Hoferer/VG Bild-Kunst Bonn).

This edition published by Burning Eye Books 2022

www.burningeye.co.uk @burningeyebooks

Burning Eye Books
15 West Hill, Portishead, BS20 6LG

ISBN 978-1-913958-33-6

The Trilogy of Surfaces and Invisibilities

CONTENTS

MONSTERS

MORBUS

À LA MODE

MONSTERS

Hell is empty / and all the devils are here.
Shakespeare, The Tempest (Act 1, Scene 2)

Monster & Maiden

I am the maiden
am the maiden
the maiden is me
who you filtered
you filtered me
I had nothing
there was nothing

left over that's me

who am I now
am I now
who? you ask me
I was the maiden
was the maiden
the maiden was me
you have filtered me

so speaks the monster

the monster is me

Carpathian

The moon is hanging distinctly between
the pines of the south.

An actress is speaking the following lines:
My love,
your beauty – I'll be candid, no closed doors in this house:
house crashbangkaput – so frightening.
You glisten,
everyone says 'pale',
from the door I heard the word
'dead'.
What do the whisperers know?

(Later, in the photos from on set, we won't be able to see you.)

Books have filled themselves with quotes and etchings about you,
all matching you only in profile.
The dilettantish man is a fearling.

Hot, ovenopen: the night breathes heated water
against me, and you,
what progress, become fog,

become rat, shadow, wolf and bat.

There's no walking beside you
while such changes occur.
I'm silent, admit, omit and permit.

'Romance is for those in the east,'
your standard line with the harsh accent
of a Romanian dissident.

GQ sent me to ask about your way with women…
C: The same as with all animals of the female sex.

And you always bite before they go to print.

Them!

The courgette's flowers are edible,
the foliage bitter, but edible.
Not to mention the fruit.
When with a blow and a flash and a blast
we became
bigger than the houses above our houses,
the flowers, the foliage, the fruit became too small.

You have to understand that.
The faster you move…

We eat you because we see you.

We hear the spiders do it that way too.

Revenants

the man
of all the maths
of slaughter
comes with counting

the doctor
eyes so pretty
comes with pictures
and comparison

men of science
men of faith
the years of one the forties
the years of the other the eighties

one granted a PhD
the other shoved in an oven
both returned

one in the dreams of thousands
the other in the dreams of thousands of others

and so two men can share a century

Rexemplar

One day it was just here,
stamped on the toes of evolution,

every pair of trousers now too small,
tore down the summerhot walls of its young days.

From Tokyo's harbour jetties
– I was still a child –
I kept lookout for the giant lizard.
I wanted to impress with my ninety-degree bow.

By the time I was ready, it was far too famous
for my greeting. Fuji's colours
sent it to the rainbow
beyond which the lizard met the moth.

I sometimes stand now at shop windows,
see those old films on TV sets
and I am six again,

ready to stick small needles into that great body,
against a silken surface, to watch
the creature that trampled the houses of my childhood.

Debutante

Fifty feet above the town
loud in bed
cold to the touch
child-in-bed-murderess
sheep in mink's clothing
affected creature, affectionate creature
seducing, singing
always in skirts too short
aging after her twentieth year
well stuffed
soon stitched up
the clitoris around the throat
of a medicine man
woman sweet
woman sour
woman with names like IKEA shelves.

She shouldn't
be driven crazy
by all of this
by all of those
for whom I am too loud.

Baby

In the first year it should
sleep as much, become as much
as possible.
What is poured into it
should leave traces,
build it up, enlarge, broaden it.
Syringes are filled
against disaster
– look at the birdie! –
the needle rammed into its arm by the doctor.
The first massive disappointment,
for the mother
watches wordlessly.
At the end of the first year
steps are due, also a word.
It must not shy from comparison
with the other miniatures.
First negotiations about ownership
and rejection, the power of gestures
and the magic of facial features
lead into the second year.
The baby receives a name
when it has become unmistakably blue or pink.
Only then is it worth the stork's
condemnation, the searching in the cabbage patch,
the nine long months of uncertainty:
fish or fowl. It is always
a thing of impossibility.

Richard the Gere

I'd use you to prove
how horrifying the years are.

From Debra Winger to Julia Roberts
to that old cop in Brooklyn –
you die more and more often
lately lame.

Or you're a solicitor for death,
advert for dying,
no longer rescuer
from the spinning mill.

Are to be rescued.
And yet – and this is shameless –
there goes that spring in your step
– still that spring –
and the particular way you hold your head.

Your voice too has to be explained
to the girls, the ones born after:
a phenomenon called desire.

King

In the zoo near the Stadt in which the races
were once segregated,
it is the crown prince of creation
who's ignoring the spectators.

Once partial to blonde women,
today he has nothing more to rue.
They have not been that blonde for quite some time.

The fifties saw him quite beside himself,
a young specimen,
full of hopes.
It's a long time since he felt moved to scale a high house
for love.

Now as then,
flies swarming round him (so many Mosquitoes, witnesses to flight),
he doesn't want to hear it said that the men
who cut off his hands
to use as ashtrays
deserve the glory,
the honour to wear the crown.

A few men and women dreamt of a future
for him and gifted him a planet
on a glittering wall
only visible in darkness,
and a language more human than his own.

It means nothing to him, being able
to name *die Banane*.

Versions

and
a boat moors
Böcklin paints a boat which moors
enshadowed
compelling
a boatman nameless
all too willing to give himself away
Hitler possessed one version
Utøya became one
island
enshadowed
compelling
a boat moors
on board a death
an advocate for crossing over
Böcklin paints a boat which moors
a boatman nameless
versions of Breivik
on board a death
peaceless
compelled
enshadowing
unshadowed
an island
and

Neglect

Children crack and break apart
at the places
we forget to smear
with time and money
where no knotted tongue
reminds us that there was something else
– but what and when – to talk about.

When we then find them,
the broken children, dry and hard
like rushes, fitting ornaments,
the mothers, the fathers are often the very last
able to look at them.

Are like the final dregs of the final dregs,
are like exhalation and fingerprints,
where no hand lay purring,
no kisses breathed
for quite some time now.

That's how it is. And there is only
a meagre amount of sandy time for anything.
When the grains run out:
good night, you ferns and rushes,
you fauns and wraiths.

Evatar

In every generation:
at least one girl in the neighbourhood
who lends the snake an ear

before quartering an apple
for lords and creation.
Their biographies for anyone who's interested:

lives as if made to be interrupted.
What's important happens in the intervals:
Lt Danny Everyman from Dallas, Fort Worth,

looks at the 'Fraulein' with honey eyes.
Let me explain, bei ihm ist sie 'scheyn'.
Mother Everyman in Dallas, Fort Worth,
is less entranced.

She comes with middle-aged double-glazed clarity,
the visibility of embroidered threads,
an incunable's colour frenzy.

Then divorce and the need
to change from Everyman to Anyman.
Who is meant to play our roles

at this level?
I worry that, us Eves,
we're all replaceable.

Golden Boy

Invited Dorian
to leave at home what he holds on to.
He wakes
at mine in a yellow room.
The effect in his words:
Midas' chamber.

At lunch
– everything strangely metallic –
he laughs and laughs.
And gold glimmers
instead of teeth
and in his iris.

Had he touched nothing,
he could have stayed.

Thus Spoke the Rabbi Loew

Show feet, hands, forehead-flat skull
and let me touch you, even narrate you.

With the Aleph for all truth and death,
breathing and chaos.

Then provide for peace in the quarter.
Draw the poisoners out of the streams,
fetch me the daughters from the beds of their defilers.

I know you are my not-yet-but-soon.

Where you step, earth resounds with heaven's power.
The way it always depends on this one sign

which makes you complete or leaves you not quite there.
My promise:

I want to bake you when everything is done.
(This will never be.)

Then we'll be potter and pot,
I your maker and your lot.

Hunter

You are bringing cake and wine, and meet the wolf.
He unzips his trousers and says:

Reach in.
He is standing right up against your car window
and you pray that he will not guess
that a button pressed in your red Ford does not automatically mean
that the wolf cannot lead you away from the path.

Finally the key slips into the ignition,
you turn it and start.
But the wolf snarls that you must stay for Grandmother's sake.
His jaws are so big, he says, all the better to eat her with
if he can't have any cake, any wine.
That's how this marriage begins, for you stay.

And he never quite eats all your cake, drinks all your wine,
always puts a bit aside in case of worse times ahead.

It is years before there is someone
who teaches you and Grandmother what is needed,
secretly, of course, after work, at a shooting range
in the woods outside the town.

But when cake and wine are then demanded
once more and you absolutely don't want to serve and to pour,
don't want to lift your skirt and spread your legs,
shots are fired.

And if he hadn't died, he'd live happily ever after.

(Years pass before a well is found,
deep enough to let things pass and fade.)

Mummy

I had asked for sleep and was cursed
when those who adopted us arrived.
As if we were children
they spoke to us in signs.
To the inventors of signs in signs!

We held our hands before our mouths
when we laughed shrilly at our visitors, partly
so the whites of our teeth would not betray our shadows.
To be subject to a king, a queen – this they knew,
like us. Only we had all been kings of our own world.
During my lifetime I had them building for my death
which neared beautifully with every day.

Whatever wears a jackal's head barks bright under the moon.
I had myself anointed, bound, belted in a cell
far beneath what can be imagined.
My entrails, memories extracted.
That's what you got out of it.
I had them engrave warnings
and wanted to sleep.
They shattered the pots of souls.
Nothing remains before eternity.

Can my fury be held against me?
Exposed and never quite awake,
I wound against myself and all who woke me.

Jaws

El tiburón, says the Mexican on the beach,
no longer eats me,
neither in one gulp nor en partes.
He doesn't even bother anymore
to watch me
each time my airbed drifts out to sea.

He has visitors all the time now and must take care,
must swim, look fierce in every photo
and yet surprise with the hunter's tenderness.

All wetsuit wearers, diving converts of the Spielberg school
know where tiburón's Achilles' weakness lies.
La nariz es tan sensible.

He's losing el respeto, the Mexican says on leaving.
You know, the dolphin too has got esta aleta,
a fin like that.

P

Sylvia and Norman share a room in a big American city. She bakes
and sometimes – overcome by sadness – she sticks her head in the
oven too. Norman wears her clothes, while in the closed ward she
doesn't really want to get better. She gets to know a veteran – the
war was just ten years ago – who tells her about Germany. She
cries and cries. When Norman visits her and they behave like man
and wife, she notices that he has been sunbathing in her bikini.
She doesn't mention this. In Sylvia's absence, Norman begins to
redecorate the apartment and to entertain. He has predilections
which he likes to share with easily frightened women. He often
thinks that, were his life a film, it could only have one title. Sylvia files
for divorce when she discovers shoes in the closet which have clearly
been worn but are not hers. He says they'd belonged to his mother.
She'd fled his father in them. Sylvia cries and writes. Norman moves
into a big house on the other side of the country.

He took the shoes with him.

Lycanthropy

you too a wee pelt
you too a wee dog
you too a wee murderer
you too a wee claw
you too a wee tooth
you too a good eater
you too a wee spring
you too a wee bullet

you too a silverling

you too a wolf

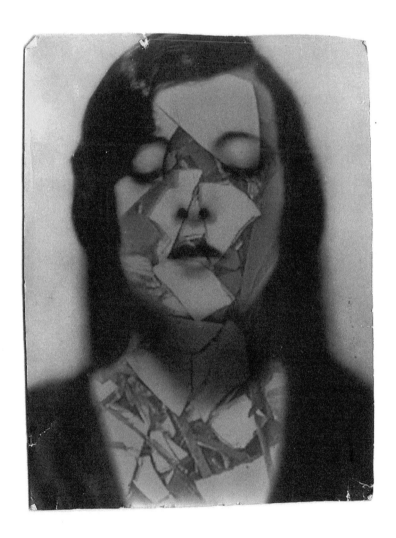

Elisabeth Fritzl

To let life happen
like the weather,
as indifferent and intricate as gravel.

They said that weather was an everyday happening.
I simply said:
That depends what day you're talking about
and where you happen to spend it.

To tell the mirror of summer:
Do you remember, mirror, mirror, on the wall?

You, my queen, are articleless – only ever one.
Next to everything something like something else.

Next to my beloved
– they said that's what you call them –
I sit, feel the far away
which I slowly but surely
choose as my abode.

There I am
unexpected. A thousand times fairer.

List for me all the shards
which I must place in this frame
so that I become visible.
Right there.

My

The lad goes right, goes left, goes forward, backward,
holds up, tidies up, is good, says nowt, just feels,
likes this, stands still, holds still, bends over, is like this,
just waits, sheds his skin, wants it, loves me,
the other,

when I tell him to.

Boy's Suit

SIZE 8

Breast 26

1

Sandmen

When out of misty haze they come to us
at night
– our houses creak and stumble, dazed –
we are held fast by nothing
and the lights flicker.
Everything wants to show us
as the beings that we are,

for to them betrayal through all the things
we made, bought, built, caught
is the truly wondrous.
For – travelling here by ship,
ploughing through the heavens' seas as captains –
they were full of curiosity about that small spirit
which even in space talks loudly of itself on tape.

Far up above the text drones on about peace and intentions
good and honourable, and it amazes them
that where they live the beings
deal in quite the opposite.
So they mark the liars where they sleep
and feed their children, where life in their owl eyes staidly
blossoms, because they tell themselves
the lie must be seen as a lure and a phenomenon,

the human species imposters
of the sons of all the worlds.

S

I say it is power,
for this it shows us,
somersaults, lightly, like a girl
or wrestles with us, a middleweight.
Paid money, this power
cannot achieve just nothing.
A riddle: how things connect
when everything you do wants to express
a horizontal feeling.
It blows the other person's breath
towards the other person into the other person's neck.
That's how power wants it, for the cycle over time
wants urgently to show itself in split cells
and to claim that one was always there before the other.
The unminged woman is also there, delicate, spooky, as in
the elements of guilt and air
which fill the pages and the pictures as alibis.
Lady Love is Lady Lust's compassionate neighbour.
But I say it is power
and with it the time to shed skins,
to give up counting hours,
to give in wishes.
Night offers excellent hunting grounds
for large creatures which hold each other down
until their breathing's rare, after
it strikes, faster than the heartbeat, to the surface.
No matter where and when the force
be with us, as was sworn to us in the star wars,
it is also hardship and destruction,
like every power which we gather
and entrust to longing.

Created

Back then Ingolstadt seemed to me a good idea.
Where they assemble things, they'll understand me.
Bodies too are vehicles,
so went my thoughts.

There'd been enough power all along;
lightning bolts strike before the Alps.
The land smoulders.

I helvetically followed rules
which I set up and did away with.
Das kleine Mensch already floating in a jar,
tragic and perfect.

There was enough material too;
madness strikes before the Alps.
The land seethes.

I'm not saying that my logic stood in the way of morals.
I call what happened magic, itself so necessary
for wisdom and wonder.

Following its assemblage it called me Vater.
I deemed the Arctic the only place
where our relationship could be resolved;
enough ice soon numbs the pain, mein Sohn.

House

Drive
Front door
Hallway
Room
Room
Room
Kitchen
Bathroom
Room
Staircase
Room upstairs
Room upstairs
Upstairs bathroom
Staircase
Attic
Boxes
Secrets

Silence
Wonky picture on the wall
Windchimes

In the cellar others, waiting

Ah-ah Machine

for Wulf Segebrecht

After the lion had died, toothless,
and the bearded woman found an admirer (hairless),
and the little men got a job in film, no fuss,
there was space in the tent.

A man wearing a cape of Italian cloth
brought her, consumptive and pale.
She walked slowly, always faltering a little,
not quite fluid somehow: her gestures, lips, words.

This way assumptions were made for the best,
the sympathy was deep,
the responses kind,
the past at this place not too closely examined.

Such a beautiful woman, and silent too!
'Heartbreaker type: ETA' stood written on her trailer,
and when the director led visitors there,
they heard an unbelievable tale.

Those times are long gone.
I purchased her. She stands at mine
between a pinball machine and a Wurlitzer
and when I show her to interested guests,

I have a coin at the ready for her ear's crooked slot,
let her tell her unbelievable tale herself.
But really she almost always just says, 'Ah, ah,'
and that leaves room for interpretation.

Traitors

Not all of the monsters described in this volume are from films or pop culture more generally. Sometimes the focus is undefined feelings, fears and traumas from everyday life. The term 'monster' itself can shift. I'm interested in who or what a monster is or can be, how it becomes a monster, and to what extent the concept 'monstrous' can be applied to everyone. I'm amazed at how positive the connotations of the term can be in English.

'Them!' – science fiction film from 1954, directed by Gordon Douglas. The first film in the subgenre of 'bug movies' which homed in on the mutation and manipulation of genetic material or insects.

'Revenants' – Freddy Krueger (fictional character from the 1980s film series A Nightmare on Elm Street) and Josef Mengele.

'Debutante' – Attack of the 50 Foot Woman, science fiction film from 1958, directed by Nathan H Juran.

'Baby' – cabbage patch: in American folklore, children aren't only brought by storks but are also found under large cabbage leaves during the full moon.

'P' – Norman Bates from Psycho, Alfred Hitchcock's 1960 psycho-thriller; Sylvia Plath.

'My' – a reaction to the film Michael (2011) by the director and screenwriter Markus Schleinzer.

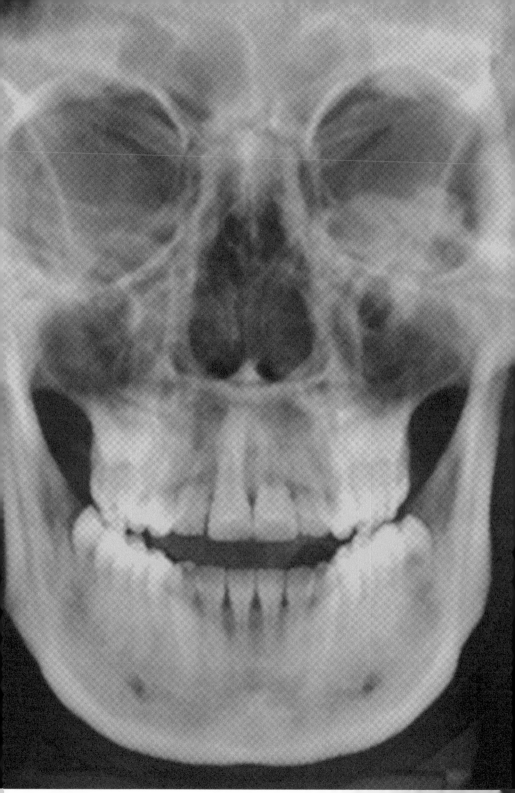

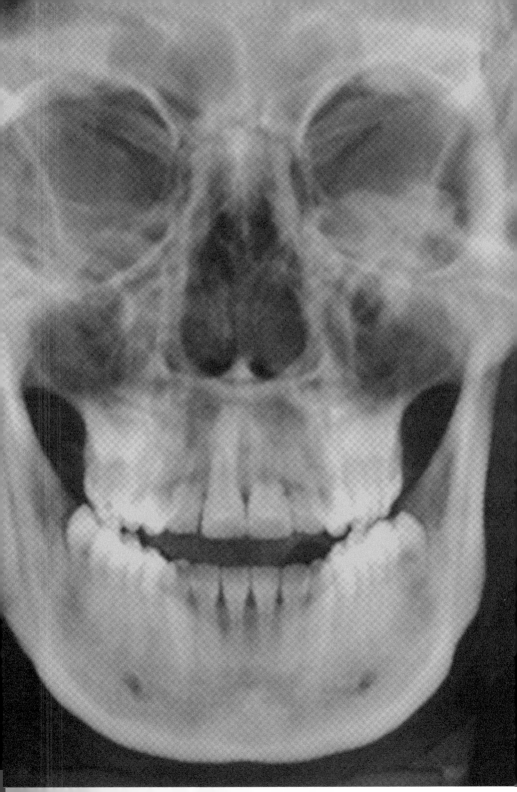

MORBUS

This book is dedicated to my grandfather George, my uncle Wolfhard and my doctors, in particular Rainer Gerstner with gratitude, as well as to the memory of Anna Schmidt.

The LORD gave, and the LORD hath taken away; blessed be the
name of the LORD.
Job 1:21

Nibbling Nashi

It guarantees the taste of roasts,
is filter, prism and preserver,
extorts bearers and admirers in equal measure.
Once indicating great plenty and abundance,
fat today is civilisation's scepticism.
In the Book of All Mugs
Slender Elf 345 writes that *fat* cannot be used as an adjective;
we ought instead to say you wear it,
like a belt collection, like the armoured animal.
Thus a person wears the raw material ungratefully
in the blood and web of its own making.
But we should know:
this fat is an astonishing friend
who also knows to draw towards us in sweet situations.
And it sustains when two, three weeks of illness,
fever, weariness befall us.
It consumes itself for us and smiles because it knows
that we'll expand and constantly
develop its estates.
Even its memory is beyond compare
for it is indicated in structure.
Where once was fat there will be fat again
and on and on it goes
in these pearapple-bodied worlds.

Educator

I am the virus which like every virus
teaches you. Understand me well:

I am obeisance, open doors, hold
them open for all kinds of visitors.
The informer is the guest
who, interlocking tenderly,
makes you blush until you leave,
caught out by our night.
The lesions then bear a name,
as I bore many, when I was still
just noise and made of smoke
which drifted upwards out of bars.
I kiss the man who kisses men.
I come in the false blood that saves.
I am in every drop, am two-faced,
split-tongued, you have my word.
So I kiss Dallas cowboys, lovely angels
and the smallest, youngest from the sleep
which they dreamt nine moons long.
And you dose acronyms
into the veins of my beloveds,
poison them in quite another way.
I am the virus which like every virus
teaches you. See the other, the other,
the always other as your wolf.
See clearly. Hear me. What I say
does not stem from me.

Place your finger
upon this mouth
when you have heard enough.

Le Petit Garçon, Platonique

for Birger Sellin, language titan

This little boy,
we would have wanted to brood him longer
in the four motherwalls, the stomachyurt,
una volta mas.
When he came, the sun was dark,
the brain eclipsed and half in shadow
the comprehension of all involved.
Who was involved?

This little boy
is an alwaysaway,
halfwayhere,
overampedanalogue,
ubiquus.
The simultaneity person of the world.
Doctorspeaksostrange.
Through him is clear how unbearable
this world for those who feel.
Searching hard we also found a word
in the thicket, under leaves and shrubs:
written savant, meaning sauvage.

The little boy,
he speaks no French. To him
the Eiffel Tower is mere steel and construction.
He's helped by keyboards
and screaming, screaming, stroke
for stroke. It is as if
someone recognised us
by that cave fire, the arching inside wall:
a shadow.
Lines ago did I not write eclipse?

Have Forgotten

have forgotten
to name like the streets
the things on which the cups
on the shelf back there in the drive
am standing naked
hair loose am wearing your ring
a man coming each day
like a what are they called
wants to rock me little one
strokes across my cheek I think
murderer you thief you leave that you
please continue never stopping
smell of talcum powder old woman
they call to me I ask them
who do you mean by that
am standing naked in the drive
have forgotten

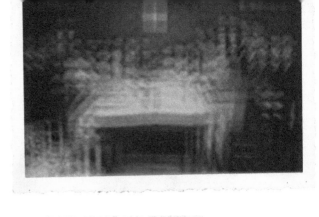

Plumbum

'…and could you describe this situation for us in your own words?'

the black dog
the leaden dress
the feathered night

the creature of fog
the quest made of questions
the questions from leather

the great silence
the total of time
the body in space

'The drug helps / the day dawns / the life: dream.'

Red Carpet Ebola

Humanity measures itself
against new pandemics.

I wish a plague on you.
You bring me blankets,
small pocks woven into them.
Our sneezes neighbourly
into our arms around each other
and every kind of kiss:
this is Judas' brotherly kiss.
I see by your hands, Thomas,
that you too cannot be trusted.

And it is always also language
which we need to send each other
anything this drastic.
The ultimatum holds. In four and twenty hours
you must vacate your place
upon this earth:

fleeing everyman,
take this way out! It will lead
to the lane behind the house
where corpses lie.

Herpeswaltz

I kiss you
Kiss me too
It meets us

I sense you
Sense me too
Stays with us

Itches you
I itch too
What to do now

I send a line
'You're still mine'

End of us

In Remembrance Of St Apollonia / I Was At The Dentist's Today

And I was wide open,
my mouth a great wound,
proof of pleasure and plenty.
Eyelids rigid with gnawing pain,
my hands holding tight like fools, yet
guessing that to hold on
wouldn't bring them anything.
Out of amalgam, skilfully,
answerlessly, the giant formed in his temple
– it was almost still the Sabbath –
a tiny blossom and buried it in a hole.
Since when have I had this hole, oh Lord? What does
it mean to carry a hole around? A nonplace, a paradise
internalised. I almost wanted to call out: this hole, it seems
to me, is me. Do not remove it from this world!

But I was long since flowered, fluoridised,
tight-lipped: a girl
before her time.

Mutabor

The error in the gene
The error in the egne
The error in the eneg
The error in the gnee
The error in the neeg
The error in in the gene
The error in in egne in
The error in in eeng inn
The error in in eeng ginn
The error in in eeng gginnn
Mutavi

Unclean

If they should call out,
clothe themselves in rags, tear at their beards,
this is according to the law.

A tiptoed glimpse was to be stolen
through the holy window
of the Lord, who doubtless
cursed them for their sins since paradise.

How else can you explain
that the places where it lives
were home, are home to so many?

An island body, pacific, peaceful,
named 'the flat land formed like a leaf'
is still a place today
where those who were removed house themselves
to their honour.

The postcard from Hawaii:
There is constant sunshine here.
It's like that film. What was it called again?
Ben-Hur.

Bye

To flutter also means to sing
for me, an all too silent creature
with wings two and
tight enthroated territory.

With radioiodine you can see me,
ultrawave tones too make
audible – large eyes
for my non-existent song.

Like crotchets, quavers, minims, semibreves
on the staves from 1 to 5,
hot, cold knots form themselves.
Belcanto doesn't want to shine.

I am the last luminous thing
when your lights cool down entirely.
I saw in Dresden's Hygiene Museum
and have believed it ever since:

I am the butterfly
that hurries after your soul.
You cannot capture, conceive, endure
what doesn't happen but for me.

Mala Aria

Anopheles, come, little beast!
Make mischief of this kind: prepare long fever nights,
crazed dreams, jolts into delirium, make talk of tropics
where lofty English coldness rules,
form memories of darkness, dances, fires!
Whatever streams from the humming to the liver, to the blood,
it knows the Tiber's banks,
the floodplained Rhine, the Panama Canal.
Colonial queen Anopheles,
you always send your troops wherever
magnifiers on the world
and blue helmets are needed.

The Heart-lung Machine Answers

Since I can think
love has been my motor.
Of course I know an Off,
which is followed by an Over,
but when you ask like that,

then I am love no matter who the person.

I am so real that I am
beyond doubt.
Should your heart no longer love,
my motor then will love you.
And if no kisses breathe anymore
then I will kiss you without pause.

I am love from demi-gods in white.

But I digress. You asked
if I could allow death. And I say:

I am that great automated love enforcement machine.
And I smile, and I duplicate like Brecht must,
as laconic as he was just.
And my smiles are never seen.

Teredo Navalis

In Stockholm, where in the sixties they salvaged a ship
from the 1600s, where you kept phoning her, always her,
her with the face of all the world,
it crawled by name across our path.

Teredo navalis –
the name spreads terror,
makes women and children fearful
and even more than them: the cap'n.

Teredo navalis –
a resident of the Vasa,
a prisoner of the elements,
a stage of existence not yet over.

Teredo navalis –
naval shipworm of up to sixty centimetres long.

As we roamed through the museum,
around a sunken major enterprise,
my parasitically occupied heart sank
with all the organs of the fleet.

Hadn't someone sewn stones into my stomach
while I was gaping wide with jealousy?

Teredo navalis –
you mariners' mawworm: in you
(like everything since then)
hides the brackish waterrotten

why.

Poliograph

My fellow Americans,
I have discovered with dismay
that my motionless legs
have driven nothing forward.

That you now kill
while seated, sending drones
when warnings on two legs
might make an impact.

Even Eleanor called it all
a blessing in disguise,
astonishing but so well
hidden until the voters'

blessing became clear:
a leader not parading
but quiet at his desk.
No shoe shuffling,

scraping hooves, impatient
for others' awe.
And how are things today?
Though we had got further?

These are the days of
common places:
the leader of the free world
a generalissmo generalissimo.

My speech on the state of the union
I address to you, as always,
seated. I had a virus.
What is your excuse?

1630 AD

The troops by Mantua: beaten.
A German again, always a German who brings destruction.
And swollen lymphs in canal vermin.

The poor turn black.
The poor decay into dampness.
It must be the steam, the people's heat.
Who can contradict with sugar in their mouth?

The city now as the silent beauty: ever more silent, ever less beauty.

The rich bleed, the poor burn to improve the situation.
If we're quite honest, we don't have it under control.
(At this point we have the Jews
pay the Christians
to lock them up.)

The senate directs, commences, enforces.
The senate is a gathering of fearful men.

He enters into their service, quite the dottore.
Venice is Helena, who no one wants to steal. To such a gift
they would say – no, thank you! The horse with troops in its
          stomach
can wait in the stable until the last trumpets.

But as with handcarts and maternal courage:
there's a business to be made here. And so: the beak and the mask!
Rub juniper, vinegar and rosemary on virgin and dotard!

Afterwards, Europe comes to know the colourful world of trade
          quite differently.
Pacts, packets, made with tiny beasts.
Rat and flea, humanity's siblings,
who are unflawed, innocence
and paradise still.

Madonna della salute, does the sight of ships itch
today like it did yesterday? The dottore will have a cure. Surely!

78

Tethered

This double vision while looking at the I
is a diagnosis
for which no glasses can be worn.

You and all the other I's,
we're in one body
hopelessly tethered to each other.

While once a man had wax dripped in his ears
so as to escape the siren song,
today it's you who bundles voices with the megaphone.

And ecstasy and noise
help overink this for the moment.
The dinner party talk in your head is constant

– tails with cummerbund for this guest,
never invited and yet a lifelong receiver for the others.

A clever film let a young woman with thirteen inner lives
be heard through Sally Field. I watched it and
thought inexorably of you.

To be the dog in your own life is the stuff of film,
but stuff of life, a means of living it is not.

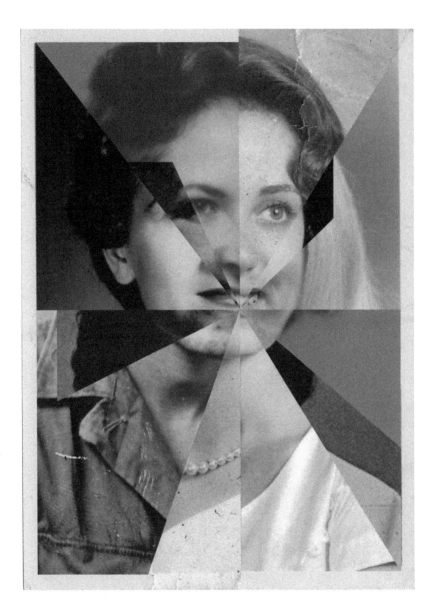

The Spanish Lady

The Spanish Lady comes from Kansas
where she's a scandal, but shhh!
Olé! She clicks her ruby heels,
wishes herself far from this Steinbeck landscape,
rallies the heartless, cowardly men of straw around her
in a tornado straight to Europe,
the Wicked Bitch of the East.

War rules there and heaven forbid
that death might now come from the west.
So everything is hushed and this becomes
black silencio on white papel.
(Everyone who'd been vaccinated died[1] – even in wonderful Oz.)

Today this girl from Kansas
is a grande dame come to visit
in history books.
But that the yellow road
lets the red shoes dance, fast-paced,
on 20 million gravestones
around the globe,
embraced by lion, tin man and scarecrow:
this, even today, is still great cinema,
death dance choreography.

---

1   A reference to the Spanish flu vaccine, which was ineffective.

Procedure

The advancing loss
of valuable genotypes
can only lead to a serious degeneracy
of all civilised nations.

With broad support
the order is given today
through the issuing of a law
on the prevention of hereditarily diseased offspring
to eliminate biologically
                              inferior genetic material.

Sterilisation should thus
effect a gradual cleansing of the nation's body
and
the annihilation

(At this point time stops, like it always does. It is quite wrong to
assume it never would. At this point, she's nineteen years old again
and a girl, now eighty. Both women coinciding in the mirror, both
unfit for the one nation's body, which made her smile. If there
hadn't been cut and scar, questions, scorn and answerlessnesses for
a while, longer than the visible signs of the period of a lifetime. We
want to discuss it precisely, this speechlessness. The mime comes
to an end where the body hand-on-heart, three crosses over the
breast, hollow hand beneath the chin, should mean home. In the
end, even an ovary is just a wee staircase to heaven for a small drop
in the big plan. We creep out of the room in which the questions
now wake and lamps shine comfortlessly bright, although the night
still deep and dark, and want to repeat with all the desolation of the
deadly language the point, for with all this arbitrariness there was
still a heart-wrenching, mind-shattering point, a point which sears in
two all that is human: sterilisation was to effect a gradual cleansing
and annihilation)

of hereditarily diseased offspring.

Venus: Vidi, Vici

The smartest minds had her for more than just one night,
lavished her with applause, French kisses, apanages.

She always gave herself the right
to announce the moment they should kneel
with, if nothing more, an itch.

The beautiful togetherness, spelt like 'death'
and its lesser form:
le petit mort.

What they were seeking between her legs?

How should I know? Yet it seems to me that men for centuries
have mastered the art of mislaying their tools.

She is by definition punishment for lust
and always allows herself to fill the space.
This disappearing space, your smallest room
between ear and other ear.
Here she makes deaf and blind and moves the furnishings around
so that you stumble over her, this bathing sister.

Cave Canem

Woofdog
Wolfmuzzle
Foaminggrrr
Carscratched
Cujo
Gooddog
Junkyard

Houndhorror
Foamingterror
Cardoor
Carwindow
Motherson
Hothot
Snapsnap
Stephenking
Spellsout
Doglatin

Should have read the sign

Traum Plus A

Join me in this charmed forgetfulness
where the birds
and the things
with the thing so thing,
you sing

thing him.
Wanted to whisper wedding,
had the snug bug,
the rug thing where things.
First kiss

and first dance.

After the trauma (Traum plus A)
saying B becomes such
a hand grenade,
so hard.

The land where only lemons bloom for us,
what is its name?
Do all the young things bleed?
Where now the young?

Oh charming, all these formulas
and the degree of my disorder:
with every more

there's thing paid in,
thing beneath the viewers' microscope.

War means that everyone wants now,
no one wants to wait.
With forty-one degrees a fevered thing's
before my mirror.

The Girls in Bergen-Belsen

Anne and Margot,
hidden so long beneath the stars,
covered with little more than a voice,
filled the lines with time
and there emerged what people
call a diary.
The book of days of one became
canon. The other
has disappeared from this earth.
Is Schwester von und Tochter von,
barely remembered as such even by the dead.
Frau Typhoid, though, still recalls
how she met the girls.
She was glad to take the bright one, so admired,
for herself. She makes for good company,
you can rhyme worlds into numbers with her.
And she's light too, light as a feather.
Although they come to a tonne
when conscience adds them one by one
to the incomprehensible total:
Margot and Anne.

White Like Muschelkalk

When somebody's ill from war
and from the bloody cash he doesn't have
and he chooses a day to kill himself
each month, then despite it all it's good
that the war is there with cane and gun and hat
and a system to take care of the widows.

That's life, a dice game with death and the devil,
both of whom are wretched players because
they have so much damn time to practice their throws.
And when someone like him – who sees himself as a sailor,

sometimes a seahorse, sometimes a man of the world –
says he will die of a white death,
then it's no joke.
It's this: empty pockets, empty belly, head full
of worries and he's a poor poet and
for eternity it will go that the good too live and
die for the high and the hangman.

Haarman's Rare Girls

The flesh of humans ought to be served warm.
It should retain its strength
to keep the neighbourhood from starving.

Just one or two ask why's 'the deer' so sticky sweet.
And the answer almost terse:

'Because it was a sugary deer with long hair and high shoes
on a dark street corner.'

Monstruation

It's true, we fear
what's never said out loud.

Particularly when it
appears as red

in darkest places.
But monthly we break

in and out of strife
and pain grace of this.

It's not your call, you
always-ever-eaters!

Accept it, man: the broad
is a gorgeous month-long monster

with lovely regularities!
If it has to release a wee egg from the ladders

and grieve for it with floods,
it may be woman.

Deal with it.
From Eve onwards

this hasn't been a thing to see as oddity or enemy.

Diagnoses

'In remembrance of St Apollonia / I was at the dentist's today' – St Apollonia, patron saint of dentists

'Unclean' – 'the flat land formed like a leaf': the former leper colony Kalaupapa

'Procedure' – Law for the Prevention of Hereditarily Diseased Offspring, 14 July 1933

'White like Muschelkalk' – 'Muschelkalk' (shell limestone): author and painter Joachim Ringelnatz's pet name for his lover

À LA MODE

These poems are dedicated to Nortrud Gomringer, who has the strictest gaze and the most well-read understanding. Nina Jäckle once declared:

'Norli, what a gorgeous brain you have!'

If this is true and I really do have a gorgeous brain, then I got it from my mum.

The majority of these poems were written in 2016 during a residency in the Goethe-Institut Villa Kamogawa, Kyoto, Japan.

'You are – just what you have been from the start.
Wear a full-bottomed wig and play the sage,
Put on high heels and strut about the stage –
You're still the same, whichever way you act the part.'
Goethe, Faust (Part 1), tr. John R Williams

Karl, Vivienne, Marc

Like three heirs of a Lear who asks
the temperatures of hearts
and dispositions, they prepare
their gifts in very different ways.
I love you as much as cloth,
I love you as much as scent,
I love you as much as leather!
The old man gives his gold to the forever young,
and where the cats now walk
the tomcats' miaow is heard from all around.

The seasons are saisons
and thus are always pincushions full of vanities.
On tailors' dummies they pin and gather,
pinch and tighten on the real thing.
Stella, Michael, Victoria, Paris can't believe
that Vera still
sews the most wedding dresses.
These are the guarantees
of life after the collection.
For several decades now the rule with questions is:
to open Vogue, Elle and Marie Claire
and only in the case of greatest doubt
– when from the bags, the bottles,
coats, vases and clothes
comes only silence – to address Anna herself.

Approach the half-lioness with courage.
And with a steak – we know who's roasting it.
And, thus appeased, perhaps the sphinx
will speak a riddle
of the coming spring: its colours,
forms, feathers and furs.
You only have to know how to read the signs
for gowns to then accept statues of Oscar,
and department store chains, the wives of oligarchs
to buy what hangs designed.

Manolo reddens soles again
and Carrie's younger sisters blog,
post, chat and comment on this new carmine.

Today, you are what you wear as rarely
as never before, for only wounded creatures
shed their skins nonstop. Thus writes one
who doesn't need to step into a wardrobe
to enter other lands.
She stands in one even before the wardrobe
and it exposes her as threadbare.

Semana Santa

When the girl vanished,
she vanished completely.
Day 1 and everybody asked someone:
Where is she? they asked, and
Where did she so completely go?
Day 2 and a few crept
awkwardly in and out of the houses.
Day 3 and cats sat in the windows.
This was no sign.
Everyone knows the Felidae
hate humans.
Day 4 and in the distance a relation
said a prayer, whispered behind her hand.
Very quietly, at night, in the bathroom
under a very harsh light.
Day 5 and two or three cases harboured
things of the disappeared. Who was she again?
Day 6 and a replacement stood,
so suddenly it shocked, in the garden under a tree.
Day 7 and it was a woman.
And as is common for women she wore a skirt.
And as is common for women she wore her hair long.
And as is common for women she wore a ring.
Beneath her veil
– as is common for women –
she became invisible.

Clutch

The bag, which has no shape
other than that of a nondescript,
far-too-large letter
and the name which – from the sound of it –
should be a seashell or a vicious
blow to the mind,
accompanies women on their night out.
Not one could fit
everything she wants in it.
Hardly anything wants to go in, and only little to stay there.
And so each time the options
must yield to the format.
No one recognises the woman
when for a joke the contents
are dissected on the table
as she powders her nose.
A lipstick: for self-defence.
A tissue: for resistance.
The mobile: for relief.
The condom: a forfeit
from the last time it wasn't used.
Not one woman has ever
closed the bag straight off.
The letter wants to be constantly updated.
The seashell only opens with reluctance.

Camouflage

in the desert
in the night
in woods
by day
waking
sleeping
with you
about you
from me
through me
Look here!
No, here!
Do you see?
I see!
almost secret
not yet quite
and not at all
do I want
to ask
should I
for you

but I become
invisible
without your
seeingme
and wantingme
gone in the fog
on paper
in cloth
in folds, sand
and without my
seeingme
almost invisible
in your hand
goes past me
that you, my heart
vastly unknown
the deception you
accept
over and over
steadfastly

Hair, Long As God Can Grow It

After the third time they all fell out.
Everyone's seen those pictures:
hair in your comb, in your hands,
in the sink, wet strands, a proper indie movie hair tragedy.

Hardly anyone knows the unfamiliar terrain
of their planet beneath its crust, beneath its coat.
How soft and hard my skull and the blood within
throb against my fingertips.

The hair of the shorn of Auschwitz
displayed in cases as far as the eye can see
prevent me from letting myself grieve
for a single parted follicle.

When the aim is to turn
as few heads as possible,
I wear a wig, a curious thing
like the lion's skin of Hercules.

Garlanding me as a gladiator
when I stand in Aldi, turn products
in my hands and check when the prophecy
proclaims the herring's end.

Oh, Rapunzel, your hair so long! And now
the one who wants to pull himself up on it.
Into your room. Does no one think of the pain
he causes you, tug by tug?

Sometimes I dream of hair:
curls and braids and strands and frizz.
And I wake with my hand between my legs.
Remembering is a knowing, growing thing.

It waits for me between the shelves.
There's many a thing I now don't need on them.
I need – here comes the big word – health.
This can't be held by mousse, nor bought with golden locks.

Lotus

Even the breaking of feet
can be found in a rulebook,
written not by torturers.
Written by lovers.
Now and again these are the same.
In time and from the earliest opportunity,
the small toe, the fourth, the third
must bend under the instep's bridge.

When do the girls run from this,
from lotus leaf to lotus leaf?

The blink before their first attempted flight:
the mothers call this 'the first steps'.
These have to be watched for.
When feet still want like stamps to press
a print onto the skin of the earth,
the hold, the surface has to be removed.

The image, quite wrongly, is one of clipped wings.
You don't have to see them grow at all;
it's much easier to start to weed when there's just roots.
The beautiful woman is the one made slow,
the *roocoocoo* derided even by the doves,
almost orthopaedic, the blood in her shoe.

Nowadays it's not the foot,
more often the promises which are broken.
For equality can only come when someone sees
how unequal things are for the other.

Farewell To The Emancipated Skirt

My skirt went to work for me today.
Held the position, A-line, neatly alphabetised.
Direct oversight, legs straightened,
the material swirling, the for and against.

In the catalogue the cut looked straighter.
During the day while walking, Skirt
rides up gradually to mid-thigh.
Why these pictures, how come so much loud liking around them?

Skirt left me wordlessly and was gone.
One double A remained for me.
In the language of cloth A + A makes a kind of circle.
I stand in trousers now, those wide ones.

When you look, they make an M or W.
In the beginning was the fig leaf.

Circus Life

Look over here! Read for yourselves!
First words are listed and then they're rhymed!

A dress like that is really a tent.
A skirt like that is like the ring.
A hat like that: this is a roof.
A shoe like that: this is a hoof.
A scarf like that is like red carpet.
A button like that is the old penny for your ticket.

A smile like that is the popcorn in its box.
A trapeze act like that is holding hands near the back.
A tiger like that is your angry father at the door.
An elephant like that: this is you after nine moons.
A clown like that is the little boy who makes you round.
A director like that, the doctor telling you to breathe.

A circus horse act: this is life then, bright plumes
upon your head and then a harness. Trot round and round
until you tire and small mice,
doves and men then make your bed.

A circus like this, it's eternal and you
just a girl, small cog clicking in the watch, ticking.
Constant and gradually driving you mad.

Gloved Family Portrait

This is the thumb;
he's in charge of money and the garden.
He wakes up early and whistles
and shakes the plums.
He picks them up,
groaning as he does so.
He carries them home,
the plums, the girls – he's a charmer, that one.
This little one here, he's
more complex. He's the youngest
and so his father loves him best.
He always stays small,
he does it all,
like a diplomat.
In prayer he meets his twin brother,
who is also small – just like him.
The next up is a go-getter;
the word 'agile' was invented for him.
The middle one is apathetic.
He stays put and often grumbles.
His neighbour is an agitator;
he helps the plum shaker and shows
the others where there's work to be done.
The other thumb is the mother in the mirrored cabinet;
she is wise and good.
When held in cow's leather in cold church,
mother and father sometimes rest against each other
like fairy tale figures, surrounded by their eight sons,
who form a roof for them, quite naturally.
Eight sisters from another hand
ought to enter here.
The fingers ought to feel around,
putting happiness into their own hands.

They'll figure things out with the in-laws.

Moustaches et Lunettes

If I draw a king,
he always has a beard.
The converse claim, though, would be incorrect.
A beard does not make a king.
What would that be like?
While the beard was growing, who would its wearer be?
A king in training? A prickly prince?
In fairy tales the man without a beard
is the woman. Wilgefortis too
enters the picture when we ask if beard
really equals man.
Woman solves the magic words, releases her hair from the tower,
bears from their skins, deer from their springs,
and states the names of little dancers
so loudly that they split in two.
On the way, she always
comes across a beard, a stranger full of follicles.
And whether he is king or servant,
hipster or hippopotamus,
in the end that's her decision too.
But vanity is settled equally.
For what the beard is to the man,
that's imitation glasses to the woman.
The world sees Adam and Eve more clearly through both.

Million Dollar Mermaid

No one swam like you.
Before you, the body was merely tossed about in water.
With luck anything raw or heavy was sanded away,
ripple effect and talented misters emerging
from the pool. Look! Mmmh! Natural Esther!
The oyster slurpers sigh so.

What Fred achieved on land beneath his soles,
you carried – back when the president was still an actor –
through the waves with front and breast stroke.
Who didn't want to plant your flag in the blue
instead of on the moon? The land of Esther.

It was Aqua! Musical! Atlantis with Weissmüller
a whole summer long. Where I live
the fishtail tends not to be appreciated. Instead it's fried.
Oh, brave queen Esther: a symbol here on my beach too?
Speedo! Spandex! Neoprene!
For the body's freedom in the cool and wet.

Did they even recognise you with clothes on?
You share the fate of all beautiful women.
We remember you by just one gesture,
just one look. If you had spoken, Esther!
Your mouth would have betrayed you,
let you drown. Albeit in Technicolour.

Nothing, Absolutely Nothing

Coquettishly it sounds from trunks, from wardrobes,
walls all full of skins: women howling, men
sighing, they have nothing, absolutely
nothing more to wear!
Perhaps they've never owned a thing.

Sheila, twelve years old, wears flipflops, shorts,
a tank top, she can describe it all
in just one sentence:
I wear this, I don't
own anything else.
She sews the clothes of the dogs,
the wolves, the sheep of other languages.

When day and night she hears and sees
nothing of the world for which she sews,
she asks herself whether she pulls threads
into the machine so as to clothe ghosts.
Ghosts of a sizeable size. She asks herself
whether there are really women who can let
their bodies grow to so much more.
Whether they really have so much to eat.

If we could see Sheila,
her nothing would weigh as much as everything.
On our imperial bodies
in their new clothes. Always new.

Dirndl

The bodice encloses the torso
just like a vase.
The breasts bloom buds
and the necks heads.
A modest hydra, think hero-boys.
The apron binds men
to the lasses when their bows
are tied beneath the heart.
If a ribbon's knotted at the back,
then God's already been brought into play.
Everybody sees in this dress
what they ought.
The velvet is a melody from space;
it too should tempt and make the men
go tender in the flesh.
Ribbons lace up the waist,
the vase's throat constricts around its own ideal.
The blouse blazing white, as if the heart's of snow
and snow a fuel,
the woman in the pot a caustic model.
In flames for home and heroes.
The skirt and its length
are, like hem and cloth,
two devotees.
The widows wear this dress
like their uniform. The lasses
wear it like a christening gown,
so proud and unblemished and esteemed,
by parents too who prize the flowers.
The bees arrive, the vase fulfils its purpose.

Hortus Conclusus Company

Where does the unicorn live?
In a place where there's also a girl.
What's it like there?
's quite nice.
The dogs in the garden are normally full.
Are sleepyheads, food all gobbled up.
The girl sews and sings and sits.
's a decoration.
The unicorn has problems with his hooves.
'nd so he has his shoes.
The sewer, singer, sitter looks after him.
Everyone just lies around the whole time.
The walls are imaginary, made up.
Made up to the nines and stuck up with it.
The dogs, sometimes, pee on them.
's disgusting.

Otherwise things are good for girl and horned creature.

The scene depicted is rare nowadays.

Something Blue

The lasses whisper:
Has he?
Everyone knows:
Yes!
This yes holds tomorrow,
every morrow and each meek and mild Amen.
The lasses like meringues are dandelion clocks,
float in for wishes and
pronounce curses only because of colours.
In this Amen she lies first of all preserved
and later buried.
Like the one with the dwarves
and the woodland creatures, but
in the fullness of the day
in a glass coffin
before all eyes
she disappears from sight.
Dissolves into a thousand lenses
like in the white alignment.
Whoever just caught
the bouquet will say:
The bride has escaped from her dress!
For the first time in his life
the bridegroom wore
a suit, which hid –
sewn into the lining – dark,
blue silk.
No bride
to know the truth there.

Elfriede Gerstl

In the midst of despair – this is the place in the web where a stitch is missing, where a thread lies not like a blade of grass but like a blade – there in the middle of the publisher's flat – this is the place where a swastika is scratched into the doorframe just beneath the mezuzah, fourth ring of the city of Vienna – I met Elfriede Gerstl.

I was so young that my word was of no significance. And she found my corpulence strange, she said so herself, what a wee soul I seemed to her, delicate, like a membrane between always seeing and always blind – this from one who was as slight as a leaf, no, as a very sharp blade on which a hair would split almost just from awe at the possibilities, almost just from fear of torture through the possibilities.

How did she get in? I do not know to tell.

Perhaps the window was ajar. And the moth Elfriede Gerstl entered the kitchen like a dream from the heyday of Escada. What was spoken? Where women once wove. Something about the Lost Clothes, the book, the one in production. The publisher, she spoke quickly and Gerstl watched me as she did. We were both silent. Never since her has someone said to my eyes that all my life I would play the role of the doll. That was the stitch of this poet.

Years later when she died, they found trailers of Chanel and the dreams of Elfriede Gerstl sewn from a precious cloth.

Barber-surgeon

For days a hole has been eating me up.
This is irony. Nothingness is plaguing me.
He should come soon with his cart,
his heavy horse in front.
He brings the pliers, potions, draughts and ointments,
grease and fat of many kinds. I stand
dissolving into pain. Folk like me
he sees in every village, but folk like him
the whole world knows by name.
To me it seems that the long trail behind the horse and cart
forms channels for the blood.
Everything takes place upon the street.
My hole becomes a well of curiosity,
my pain spectaculum, the woman
in which the two now fight: a sideshow.
I do not care. He arrives like Cronus,
who gnaws at me for hours
until he understands that only the young
are tender to consume.
Don't share your cherries with hole-filled folk like me.
The stones like cannonballs hurled
right at the fortress, once all white.
Enemy takeovers all the time!
That I recognise myself
is miraculous, deprived of mirrors
as I am.

Uniform

In uniform the stooped walk tall.
The more metal on one's collar, the higher
one's ideals – thus a veteran
might explain the outfit
to the grandkids.
Such old values and their echoes
in the stripes, in the foliage
which rustles and whispers of equality.
No more than whispers if no one
sees himself when looking at the other.
When I hold myself against the light and so
against the others, I examine myself
and in this lies the will
to encounter me again and again.
The uniform holds the knowledge
of the scope of each spirit
and the measurability of bodies with designs
that have been clearly framed since Darwin.
It is the only form binding everyone and
wanting, in doing so, to hold them. No one may grow,
or at least only in the sizes
available in camp.
The picture: in some rooms it wears
a black ribbon embracing
the corner – sleek and gleaming but also tight.
The widow is handed the national flag
when her spouse lies in honour beneath the earth.
All of the buttons then are
very dark bright stars, all of one form.

Geisha

The wide silk wings this woman has,
embroidered and hemmed with words
for grace, hemmed in such a way
that inside, outside,
like siblings in their youth,
appear together in the portrait
when she stands bowed, my gaze
resting on her collar and then deeper, on her skin.

She wears the gown's expanse
girded, as if this way she is encircled,
part of this geomagnetic world
and really from a kingdom far from all hardship.

The steps, each separate step
swiftly treads a protocol onto the asphalt
of the narrow lanes. It tells
of yarn and scent, talents
between promises, silence and the flattery
of an eye touched with red.
The cherry blossom on her lips opens only for song.
The smile, expensive for the living earned,
is taken as a seal for the word.

Still a young woman, she sees herself as old
just the next week, when
sake opens her lips, here and here.

Maybelline 306

With this colour
I paint for war, display, perform
a fore. Yes, that is part
fury, part whore, who does well when you
regard her, feel her, rent her.
I buy in bulk and without cease
she screams and smacks. Like good colour does
when left to take effect
without a word.
Leave the house without colour
and you'll stay circumstantial, crème anglaise, beige concentrate.
At least with painted lips it's marked
where could be spoken of an I.
Such a mouth is – like the body –
also just a place to stay, I tweeted,
and women watched in horror to see their men
hearting this.

Little Black Something

You clothe everyone drawn to your pelt.
God, nature is a capricious man
with a fur farm.
Cages full of fools.
Or what's the mother's word for the ones
who didn't flee but ran towards the feed?
When someone's born behind bars
they see everything with that pattern.
And freedom is the wild speculation
of feverish new inmates.
At night, when nature sleeps,
your own dreams gnaw.
In them four legs test the forest floor
under their soft pads. By day, then,
night tugs at your tail,
nature literally fleeces the slumberers' wee ears.
Dreamers' Destiny hangs above the shops
in which indulgence from a guilty conscience
can be bought.
It's seldom said
the whole thing isn't worth this.
The little black number now hangs from a collar.
A shadow, a charmer. A puppet.
There's a name for all of them.
It melts moorishly, bitterly,
has for eternities spoken itself on tongues,
marked with colonial colour:

slaves.

A Shirt Made Of Hair In The Walking Dead, Season 5

When the priest spoke of his disquiet,
we thought it was a matter of the world, his relationship
with God, creation. We vaguely thought of his digestion.

He rubbed his arms and bit his lips,
his face contorted in pain.
An image! The Lord's likeness hung in memory, his arms outstretched.

He gasped for breath. With this especially
precious – because fought for – air, he explained to us:
himself. And we heard: him. And didn't understand: how?

In a world after the apocalypse – yes, these are the times
in which the dead warm up – a sense still held him,
the memory of neglect towards the living.

Conscience. That's what we say. It is conscience
showing itself here. He has stopped like a clock.
In malaise, which is a garden without embellishment, endless in time.

Wears a penitential shirt of hair, finely woven from animals
and humans, from elements of creation for whose forgiveness
he hopes. His flayed skin bleeds into the fabric.

And suddenly he is: him, really Jesus on the cross. No longer just
          an image.
What God created he makes bleed.
If a hairshirt like this had a pattern,
it would be of capillary concentric conception.

Poppins' Bottomless Bag

The wind changed and a clasp – how ironic! –
released the bag.
And as she sang, the things
fantastically emerged from it:
a goldfish bowl, an umbrella,
and all the things to fill the syllables.
With each piece that became visible
her departure was made manifest.
I understood this woman never loves you,
that she leaves first and without tears,
makes you fall wretchedly in love
with her lullabies, her lips.
She gives you medicine and smiles its bitterness far away.
She's no doctor. She's the thief
of your childish heart, yielding fixed interest
and sugary in the bank.
That's how Father wants it.
Mother is saving you from wrong,
which means that she has little time.
And that leaves only this woman, who you love
like none other.
Who packs her bag, that bottomless bag,
again with goldfish bowl
and umbrella, and you ask
once the pictures are all finished
and the cut complete
if you and your brother wouldn't fit in too.

At which she laughs, closes her bag
and, because the wind is changing,
goes far away, to poison other children
with her sugar, her sweetness.
Nanny Poppins:

you owe me my childhood.
Not to mention the glimpse
of the abyss.

Ed's List

Beautiful rubbish bin
Comfortable seats thanks to handy covers
Exquisite bedpost ornaments
Exceptional corset
Stunning leggings
Eye-catchers! Masks!
Finely worked belts
Curious pull-cord for the blind
Radiant lampshade

From skin, cartilage, bones
Elaborately finished, much discussed collection
Paid for in full with sanity
Also costing some their lives

Fox Spirit

they call me. Also:
tooth gnawing at wedding rings.
You shouldn't have joined in,
should have stood firm.
Not my fault, never my indiscretion.
My ochre coat, such January embers.
I transform in the dog days,
am a woman aflame
in a Bluebeard house.
Go ahead and hunt me, women
of the men I lead
into the woods and the lakes they hide.
Like all women in these myths
I know secrets of the lips,
eyes, sinews. My sharp teeth
have to chatter
when I am cold and want to entice someone.
They are all warm-blanket manufacturers
when a beauty's barely moving for the cold.
And when they howl and ask, 'Say, what's your name?'
I say, 'Vulpecula.'
For that way, Latin hides me from the dogs.

Silkworms

for Daniela Hoferer

The ability to render what's recorded in bare threads.
Not like a precocious child. Like the silkworm: bodily!
The chameleon even. It moves you and enchants itself.
Because we now know each other across countries,
she asks me if the new invisibility of scars
will flow into the poem. I say: as a fragment, perhaps.
As spider's leg, lizard's tail, ox's horn.
Everything that grows back is a part of this world. So too her thread.

As an embroiderer she pierces minus into plus in the system of
        coordinates,
binds worlds through threads, is a student of the fates,
the horizon's diplomat.
Someone like her embroidered a pillow with a love letter,
which doubled as biography. (Neither tend to be encouraged.)
Thus the stitches are always the same. Only those who pierce them
        differ.
She tells me that needles must be chosen precisely,
thread and type of stitch dictate. I think, foil or rapier?
To perpetuate streams of images is her gallery wall concept:
guided by thread through the labyrinth. Kaleidoscopes emerge.

A hole in the world can be pierced so quickly. To fill it,
to do so again and again, that's our lot.
The silkworm eats holes and absences into the world,
filling herself up on them.
Eating white makes her wise;
eating black, depressed.
In her and from her the universe grows and threads itself,
no more than absence and pattern, Hawking says.

I wanted to say this:

Her gaze pierced me, threaded me with skill.
A camel, me, through her eye.

Translator's Note

Translation always takes place in conversation – with authors, editors, colleagues, friends. My warm thanks go in particular to Nora, for her generous sharing of words and ideas, and to the whole of the Burning Eye team, for taking such good care of the translations.

A number of these translations were completed during residencies at Cove Park and the Literarisches Colloquium Berlin – thanks too to the teams who made these residencies possible and to the colleagues and swimming buddies who made them joyful.

Lightning Source UK Ltd.
Milton Keynes UK
UKHW051251071022
410092UK00013B/54